George Washington
And His Right-Hand Man

Stephanie Kraus

Consultant

Diana Cordray
Manager, Education Center & Youth Programs
George Washington's Mount Vernon

Publishing Credits

Rachelle Cracchiolo, M.S.Ed., *Publisher*
Conni Medina, M.A.Ed., *Managing Editor*
Emily R. Smith, M.A.Ed., *Content Director*
Seth Rogers, *Editor*
Robin Erickson, *Senior Graphic Designer*

Teacher Created Materials

5301 Oceanus Drive
Huntington Beach, CA 92649-1030
http://www.tcmpub.com
ISBN 978-1-4258-6356-2
© 2017 Teacher Created Materials, Inc.

Table of Contents

The First President. 4

Life in the Colonies. 6

Forming a Government 14

Leading a Nation. 20

Final Goodbyes 24

A Great Team. 28

Glossary. 30

Index 31

Your Turn!. 32

The First President

George Washington was one of America's Founding Fathers. He served his country as a general, a president, and an inspiration. Washington's life and **legacy** have been well preserved. He was known for his good character and strong **morals**. These values helped Washington during the Revolutionary War. They also helped him lead a new nation as its first president. He was the "Father of His Country."

Experts call Washington one of the best presidents in history. But, it is also important to remember that he was a son, a brother, a husband, a stepfather, and a friend. He was loyal but could be cold when crossed. His hobbies included breeding dogs, foxhunting, and ballroom dancing. Washington did not seek attention or power. He had a quiet confidence. Yet, he also had doubts about his ability to lead the country.

Washington is an **icon** of the United States. To truly understand U.S. history, it's important to learn about Washington's life and the people who stood by him.

Washington Monument in Washington, D.C.

Washington hunting with his dogs

Nothing But a Hound Dog

Washington loved dogs. He bred hound dogs to accompany him on hunts. Some people say he bred the first American foxhound. Washington showed his sense of humor by naming his dogs Mopsey, Sweet Lips, Madam Moose, and Vulcan.

American Roots

Washington's great-grandfather was a merchant who sailed from London, England, to Virginia in 1656. His ship, the *Sea Horse*, needed repairs before it could sail back to England. While waiting, Washington met his future wife, Anne Pope. When the ship was ready to sail, Washington stayed behind and started a new life as a farmer in Virginia.

Life in the Colonies

George Washington was born on February 22, 1732. He was born in Virginia. This was one of the thirteen British **colonies** that would become the United States.

Washington grew up in Virginia with eight siblings. He was a good student, but after his father's death, his family could not afford to send him away to school. So, he became a **surveyor**. He spent a lot of time outdoors and was skilled at horseback riding and hunting.

Washington wanted to join the British Royal Navy, but his mother wouldn't let him. She wanted her son to stay close to home. When he was 21, Washington joined the local colonial army.

Young Washington tells his father about the cherry tree.

What's in a Name?

From the name of the French and Indian War, you might think that the French fought the Indians. Actually, the war was mainly between the French and British. Both sides had American Indians fighting with them.

The Cherry Tree Myth

There is a famous story about Washington chopping down his father's cherry tree as a young boy. When his father asked about it, Washington said, "I cannot tell a lie ... I did cut it with my hatchet." In fact, Washington's first biographer may have invented this story. He wanted to illustrate Washington's honesty.

Washington on horseback during
the French and Indian War

The French and Indian War

In 1753, American Indians and the French started to build forts in the Ohio Valley. The British colonists became angry. They believed that the land belonged to them.

The governor of Virginia sent the young Major Washington to tell the French to leave, but they refused. A few months later, Washington returned with troops. They attacked the French post and killed the leader. However, the colonists were then surrounded by the French at Fort Necessity. This was the beginning of the French and Indian War.

destruction of tea at
Boston Harbor

After the War

In 1763, the French **surrendered** to the British. The French and Indian War was over. Washington described his Ohio Valley battles in *The Journal of Major George Washington*. His leadership and bravery made him famous.

After the war, Washington returned to his Virginia plantation, Mount Vernon. He married a young, wealthy **widow** named Martha Dandridge Custis. She had two children, Jacky and Patsy. Washington was active in local politics. However, he was ready to live the quiet life of a farmer.

Too Many Taxes

Back in England, King George III had to figure out how to pay the **debts** of the costly war against the French. The king decided to tax the colonists. The Stamp Act taxed paper documents. Then, the Townshend Acts taxed tea, glass, lead, paper, and paint.

In 1770, colonists in Massachusetts protested these taxes. They yelled and threw rocks at British soldiers. The soldiers fired their weapons. Five colonists died in what was called the Boston Massacre.

Three years later, the British passed the Tea Act. According to this law, the colonies could only buy tea from a British company. Colonists protested by dumping 342 chests of tea into Boston Harbor. This event became known as the Boston Tea Party.

Busy Bee

Martha Custis (above) described herself as an "old-fashioned Virginia house-keeper, steady as a clock, busy as a bee, and cheerful as a cricket." Her life was full of tragedy, but she was "determined to be cheerful and happy."

Red for the Rich

British soldiers wore red coats and were called Lobsterbacks or Red Coats. During this era, only rich people could afford expensive dyes. In many places, only royalty wore dark colors such as purple.

9

For a Good Cause

In 1774, the First Continental Congress met in Philadelphia, Pennsylvania. There were 56 **delegates**. They discussed what to do about the British. They decided to send a document of **grievances** to the king. It stated that war could be avoided if the king treated them fairly. The king never responded. Less than a year later, the Revolutionary War began in April 1775.

Congress chose Washington to lead the new Continental Army. Washington wrote to his wife saying that he did not want to leave his family. But, he felt it was his duty to help the cause. He would not return to Mount Vernon for eight years.

Thief in the Night

One night in 1775, Alexander Hamilton and other soldiers attempted to steal British cannons in Manhattan. British ships opened fire on them. But, Hamilton and his men still managed to steal 21 cannons.

A Clean Break

On July 4, 1776, Congress adopted the Declaration of Independence. This document explains why the colonies broke ties with the British. It also grants key rights to American **citizens**.

colonial artillery company in New York

Hamilton Joins the Cause

Around the same time, Alexander Hamilton joined the revolution. Hamilton was born in the West Indies. When he was 14, he wrote, "I wish there was a war." Within two years of his 1773 arrival in America, there was.

Hamilton attended King's College in New York City. He was smart and gave speeches about why people should join the revolution. He also started writing about politics.

He joined a **militia**. Soon, he became a captain in the Continental Army. During early fighting in New York and New Jersey, Hamilton's bravery did not go unnoticed.

Alexander Hamilton

The First and Second Continental Congresses were held at Carpenters' Hall in Philadelphia, Pennsylvania.

Part of the "Family"

During the early battles, Hamilton caught the attention of General Washington. In 1777, Washington asked Hamilton to be his **aide-de-camp.** Hamilton wanted to be a part of the action. He didn't like the idea of working at a desk. But, he accepted the job with Washington.

The two men worked together for the next four years. Hamilton put Washington's thoughts and plans into writing. Hamilton also offered advice to bring order to the army. He became Washington's right-hand man.

Washington and Hamilton meet on a battlefield during the American Revolution.

Bumping Heads

Even though the two men had different personalities, they made a great team. Hamilton was bold and emotional. Washington was quiet and reserved. He had good judgment in tough situations.

The two men were not always friendly to each other. One time Hamilton kept Washington waiting for a meeting. Washington said, "I must tell you, sir, that you treat me with disrespect." Hamilton quit his job. He wrote that he never felt friendship for the commander. However, Hamilton eventually returned to service because he believed in the war. He regularly asked Washington to let him lead men in battle. Washington would finally let Hamilton lead troops at the Battle of Yorktown.

Washington meets with advisors at his house in New York.

Side by Side

Staff aides lived and worked together. Many developed friendships and nicknames. Hamilton was nicknamed "The Little Lion." Hamilton addressed Washington as "Your Excellency."

Still Fighting

At Yorktown, Hamilton led the 1st Battalion, 5th Field Artillery Regiment. This unit is still active in the army. It is the oldest serving active duty unit in the United States military.

Forming a Government

The French sent weapons and ships to support the colonists. With their help, the American forces were able to win the Battle of Yorktown. After three weeks of fighting, the British surrendered in 1781. It was the final battle of the Revolution.

In 1783, the two sides signed a peace **treaty**. It said the United States of America was an independent country. Now a plan was needed for how to govern the new nation.

Hamilton and Washington went their separate ways after the war. Washington retired from the army and returned to Mount Vernon. Hamilton went back to New York where he became a lawyer. The two men met again in 1787. Both were part of the Constitutional Convention in Philadelphia.

Famous Lines

Patrick Henry was famous for saying "Give me liberty or give me death!" to urge colonists to fight against the British. He did not like the secret closed-door meetings of the Constitutional Convention. He proclaimed, "I smell a rat!"

Franklin in Paris

In 1776, Benjamin Franklin went to France. His goal was to enlist the help of the French in the war. He was very well received by the French upper class. He lived in France for nine years before returning home. France's involvement in the war is almost certainly due to Franklin.

Paris, France

The British surrender at Yorktown.

Signing the Constitution

Hamilton was one of the driving forces behind the Constitutional Convention. One year earlier, he had been part of the small Annapolis Convention. He convinced the few Annapolis delegates to call for a larger meeting. The meeting needed delegates from all thirteen states. Hamilton wanted laws to give the United States a strong central government. He didn't want to simply change the **Articles of Confederation**. He wanted to create new laws for the new country.

On the other hand, Washington had to be convinced to attend the convention. He had hoped to live a quiet life with his wife. But Mount Vernon was rarely quiet. Leaders like James Madison and Henry Knox visited. They convinced Washington that he was important to the success of the convention. Washington agreed to attend for the good of the United States. He was unanimously voted president of the convention.

Delegates from the states came together. They needed to decide how the new country would be run. They wanted a government that could protect people but still give them their rights. The men worked for four months and fought on many topics. The Constitution was signed on September 17, 1787. The next step was for nine of the thirteen states to **ratify** it.

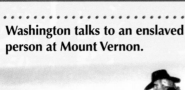

Washington talks to an enslaved person at Mount Vernon.

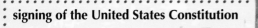

signing of the United States Constitution

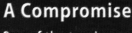

A Compromise

One of the turning points in the Constitutional Convention was the Three-Fifths Compromise. Every enslaved person counted as three-fifths of a person when determining population. This gave the South more delegates in the House of Representatives.

Branches of Power

The delegates created a system with three branches of government. The legislative branch makes the laws. The executive branch enforces the laws. And, the judicial branch interprets the laws. This system of checks and balances makes sure that no one branch has too much power.

Read All About It

The Federalist Papers was a collection of 85 essays. The essays were printed in New York newspapers. The Constitution was confusing to people. The essays explained it in understandable ways. At first, the authors were **anonymous**. Later, the authors were identified as Alexander Hamilton, John Jay, and James Madison. These essays were eventually reprinted all over the country.

To be ratified, the Constitution needed nine of the thirteen states to vote in favor of it. This was not an easy process. It took ten months to get the needed votes. Finally, a **Bill of Rights** was added to the document. Then, the rest of the states voted in favor of the Constitution. It became the law of the land.

The Federalist Papers

Towering Above

Washington's legacy is not the only thing people have to look up to. At six foot two inches (1.9 meters) and 200 pounds (90.7 kilograms), Washington was one of our largest presidents.

All in Favor

Washington is the first and only United States president to be unanimously elected. One candidate did come close. James Monroe won all except one of the electoral votes in 1820.

The Votes Are In

When it came to choosing the president of the new country, all the delegates felt Washington was the right person for the job. Washington knew he would have to establish strong values for the new country. He wanted to unite the states and serve as a strong model for future presidents.

In 1789, he was sworn in on Wall Street in New York City. This was the nation's capital at the time. He was greeted with cheers, church bells, and music when he arrived for his **inauguration**.

Federal Hall

Washington's First Inaugural Address to Congress

Leading a Nation

Washington realized that leading the new nation would be difficult. He did not want to push the limits of his power. He looked to his staff for help. Rather than make decisions on his own, he created a small council of men to help him. This group was called the **cabinet**. Washington asked Hamilton to be the first secretary of the treasury. Thomas Jefferson was the first secretary of state.

Washington also wanted Hamilton to help create the tone of his administration. What should the president be called? How would the new country pay their debts? Where should the president live?

Hamilton wanted to set a "pretty high tone." Two suggested titles were "His Highness" or "His Exalted High Mightiness." But Washington chose a less formal title. He wanted to be called "Mister President."

George Washington

Thomas Jefferson

Henry Knox

At Odds

The nation had a lot of debt from the war. Hamilton asked Washington to approve a national bank to help pay off those debts. Other cabinet members, such as Jefferson, opposed this idea. From the very beginning, Hamilton and Jefferson disagreed on the nation's path. It's possible that this is why Washington had them on his staff. They offered very different points of view. Jefferson thought the states should be able to govern themselves. Hamilton supported the idea of a strong federal government.

Odd Man Out

John Adams (above) was Washington's vice president. However, he was rarely asked for advice on major issues. Washington consulted with his cabinet members instead. Even so, Adams kept a polite relationship with Washington during their time in office together.

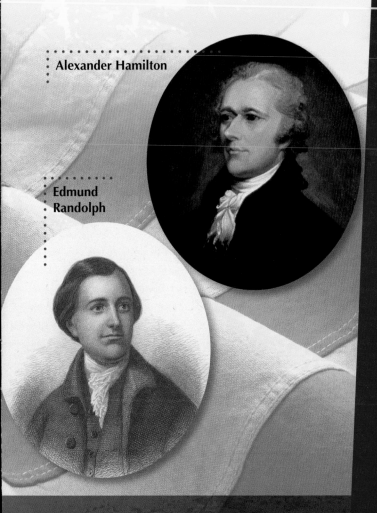

Alexander Hamilton

Edmund Randolph

Cabinet

Hamilton and Jefferson were not the only people in Washington's cabinet. There were four members in total. Henry Knox was secretary of war, and Edmund Randolph was the attorney general. Both men had worked with Washington during the war.

Hamilton vs. Jefferson

Hamilton wanted to create the First Bank of the United States. He thought it would improve the nation's credit. Then the government could help pay off the nation's war costs. The bank also would create a common currency—the U.S. dollar. Hamilton called his plan the Assumption Bill.

Jefferson thought this plan took power from the states. He told Washington that Hamilton was trying to make America more like Great Britain. Washington didn't know much about finances, but he trusted Hamilton.

Saving Face

Hamilton's face is on the $10 bill. He is one of three non-presidents to be featured on U.S. currency. Benjamin Franklin is on the $100 bill, and Salmon Chase (U.S. senator, governor, and Supreme Court Justice) is on the $10,000 bill.

Don't Go!

For ten years, Philadelphia was the nation's capital city. Washington, D.C., was being planned and built. The people of Philadelphia wanted to keep the capital. So, they offered Washington a mansion to try to get him to stay.

Hamilton and Jefferson

At the same time, the location of the nation's capital was being debated. Some people wanted the capital to be in Philadelphia or New York. Others pushed for it to be in the South. It was Washington's decision to make. So, he put it up for a vote. Whichever location received the most votes would be named the nation's capital.

At a private dinner, Jefferson, Madison, and Hamilton discussed both matters. They made a secret deal. Jefferson and Madison would get southern support for Hamilton's financial plan. In return, Hamilton would sway New Yorkers to support moving the capital to the South. On July 16, 1790, Washington, D.C., was named the nation's capital.

First Bank of the United States in Philadelphia

Final Goodbyes

Washington thought about retiring after his first term. But, he was worried about the country. Jefferson said the union would fail without his leadership. Washington was **reelected** in 1792. John Adams was the vice president again.

During his second term, Washington faced some tough decisions. He was getting questioned about the national bank. The politics began to wear him down.

Washington also had to decide if the United States should get in the middle of a war between Great Britain and France. Hamilton said the new country should stay out of it. Jefferson argued that the nation owed the French for their help during the Revolution. Once again, Washington agreed with Hamilton to stay **neutral**.

Hamilton resigned in 1795. He returned to being a lawyer. But, he still served Washington. He helped Washington write his famous Farewell Address in 1797. Washington asked fellow Americans not to judge him too severely. He also warned the country to stay out of foreign wars.

Washington and Martha returned to Mount Vernon. He wrote letters and spent time with his family. He and Martha finally had the chance to retire and settle down.

Washington's Farewell Address

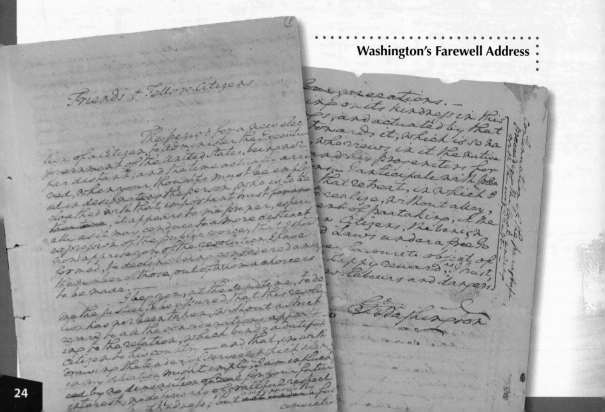

Washington relaxes at Mount Vernon.

Mount Vernon

Choosing Sides

Jefferson and Madison started the Democratic-Republican Party. They believed the states should have strong rights. Hamilton was a member of the Federalist Party and believed in a strong central government. Washington did not approve of political parties.

The Affair

Hamilton may have become a U.S. president if he hadn't started a relationship with a married woman. He tried to clear his name by writing about it in newspapers, but his public image was ruined. Through it all, Washington refused to turn against Hamilton and continued to support him.

Loss of a Father

Washington died on December 14, 1799, at the age of 67. His death was mourned all around the country. Even those who disagreed with his politics knew what a great loss this was for the country.

Washington was humble until the very end. He signed his will as *George Washington, of Mount Vernon, a citizen of the United States*. Hamilton would soon learn how hard political life could be without Washington's guidance.

Washington's funeral procession in Philadelphia

Burr shoots
Hamilton in a duel.

Final Thoughts

The last letter that Washington ever wrote was to Hamilton. It was written two days before he died. In it, he complimented Hamilton, who wanted to open a military academy at West Point.

Battle with Burr

The election of 1800 ended in a tie between Thomas Jefferson and Aaron Burr. The choice between the two men was left up to the House of Representatives. Many looked to Hamilton to tell them who to vote for. Although he disagreed with Jefferson on almost every issue, Hamilton said to vote for Jefferson. Jefferson stood for what he believed in. Hamilton could not say the same about Burr. Jefferson won and became the third president. Burr was vice president.

When Burr ran for governor of New York, Hamilton spoke against him again. Burr lost that election as well, and he blamed Hamilton. In 1804, Burr challenged Hamilton to a duel. Burr shot Hamilton, who died the next day.

Great Misfortune

Jefferson did not attend Washington's funeral. Over the years, Martha Washington grew to dislike Jefferson because of his frequent attacks on her husband. When Jefferson was elected as president, Martha commented that it was "the greatest misfortune our country had ever experienced."

A Great Team

Washington and Hamilton worked closely together for more than 20 years. Both men understood each other. Together they achieved many amazing things. They fought in the Revolutionary War. They helped write the Constitution. And above all, these two men valued honor and duty to their country.

Hamilton had great ideas about how to establish a strong nation. Washington knew how to put those ideas into action. Washington relied on Hamilton's advice. They set the stage for America's first presidential administration.

It's clear that both men respected one another. But, they also had many disagreements. That may be why their relationship worked so well. Despite these differences, they worked together to find solutions. And through it all, they remained loyal to each other.

Washington and Hamilton prove that the people by your side can have a big impact on your life. These Founding Fathers dealt with many hurdles in building a new nation. By working together, they created a solid foundation for America.

Second to None

Patriot Henry Lee described Washington after his death. He said, "First in War, first in peace, and first in the hearts of his countrymen, he was second to none in the humble and endearing scenes of private life."

Virtuous Leader

Hamilton wrote of the commander, "He consulted much, pondered much, resolved slowly, resolved surely." After Washington's passing, Hamilton wrote, "I have been much indebted to the kindness of the General. If virtue can secure happiness in another world, he is happy."

perfect Union, establish
Blessings of Liberty to ourselves
JULY 4, 1776.

Glossary

aide-de-camp—a military officer who assists another high-ranking officer

anonymous—not named or identified

Articles of Confederation—the original governing document that was replaced by the Constitution in 1789

Bill of Rights—the first ten amendments to the Constitution

cabinet—a group of advisors to the president

citizens—members of a state or country

colonies—areas that are controlled by or belong to a country and are usually far away from it

debts—money owed to someone or something

delegates—people chosen by a group to represent the whole group's interests

grievances—complaints

icon—a famous person or thing that represents something important

inauguration—a ceremony where someone, such as a new president, is put into office

legacy—anything handed down from the past to future generations

militia—a group of people who are not part of the armed forces of a country but are trained like soldiers

morals—a person's beliefs about what is right and wrong

neutral—describes a person or country that does not support either side of an argument or war

ratify—to make something (like a contract) officially valid through votes

reelected—to have elected (someone) who was already in office

surrendered—to have given up power or control to another upon demand

surveyor—someone whose job is to measure and examine an area of land

treaty—an official agreement that is made between two or more countries or groups

widow—a woman whose husband has died

Index

Adams, John, 21, 24

Annapolis Convention, 16

Articles of Confederation, 16

Assumption Bill, 22

Battle of Yorktown, 13, 14

Bill of Rights, 18

Boston Massacre, 9

Boston Tea Party, 8–9

Burr, Aaron, 27

colonies, 6, 9–10, 14

Constitution, 16–18, 28

Constitutional Convention, 14, 16–17

Continental Army, 10–11

Federalist Papers, The, 18

Federalist party, 25

First Bank, 22–23

First Continental Congress, 10–11

Founding Fathers, 4, 28

Franklin, Benjamin, 14, 22

French and Indian War, 6–7, 9

Henry, Patrick, 14

Jefferson, Thomas, 20–25, 27

King George III, 9

Knox, Henry, 16, 20–21

Madison, James, 16, 18, 23, 25

Monroe, James, 18

Mount Vernon, 9–10, 14, 16–17, 24–26

Randolph, Edmund, 21

Revolutionary War, 4, 10–12, 14, 24, 28

Stamp Act, 9

Tea Act, 9

Three-Fifths Compromise, 17

Townshend Acts, 9

Washington, D.C., 4, 22–23

Washington, Martha Dandridge Custis, 9, 24, 27

Washington's Farewell Address, 24

Your Turn!

Many portraits of George Washington feature him wearing his military uniform. Why might an artist choose to paint him dressed this way rather than in regular clothes? The portrait above was painted in 1788, five years after the American Revolution ended. Looking closely at the details of the portrait, what do you think the artist wanted to convey about George Washington? Now, draw a self-portrait. Include clothing and props that convey the image that you would like others to have of you when they view it.